This book belongs to:

MY FIRST DICTIONARY

Illustrated by Jessica Stockham (Beehive Illustration)
Design by Design Principals, Warminster

This is a Parragon Publishing book
This edition published in 2003

Parragon Publishing
Queen Street House
4 Queen Street
BATH, BA1 1HE, UK

ISBN 0-75257-763-8
Printed in China

MY FIRST DICTIONARY

Written by Betty Root

p

Using this dictionary with your child

This colorful picture dictionary will be enjoyed by all young children. The very young will love to share it with an adult, talking about the lively pictures and giving names to the pictures they recognize.

Children who have just started to read will use the dictionary to understand the meanings of words and how to spell them. Some words may be unfamiliar; introducing those words will extend and enrich both spoken and written vocabulary.

The words in this dictionary are in alphabetical order. By using this book frequently, children will begin to remember where letters occur in the alphabet. This is a very useful skill. For each word there is an illustration, together with a simple definition and a sample sentence to help explain the meaning further. Care has been taken to ensure that the illustrations give the right clues to the sample sentences.

Children will want to return to this dictionary again and again because it is both attractive and satisfying. The joy of using the dictionary will help children learn how to read many words and how to spell them. They will also learn that the world of words can be wonderful!

Betty Root

Aa Bb Cc Dd Ee
Ff Gg Hh Ii Jj
Kk Ll
Mm Nn
Oo Pp

Contents

Qq Rr
Ss Tt Uu Vv
Ww Xx Yy Zz

Aa

airplane
An airplane is a machine with wings. It flies in the sky.

People ride in airplanes to get places quickly.

alphabet
The alphabet is the name for all the letters that we use to write words.

There are 26 letters in the alphabet. The first letter is a.

alligator
An alligator is a big, long animal. It has thick skin and sharp teeth.

Alligators use their long tails to swim in lakes and rivers.

angry
An angry person is someone who is upset or annoyed.

Baby Bear is angry because someone has eaten his food.

animal

An animal is something that is alive and can move around. Plants are not animals.

Monkeys, parrots, snakes, and people are animals.

asleep

When you are asleep you rest with your eyes shut. You do not know what is going on around you.

You are asleep at night in your bed.

ankle

Your ankle is a part of your body. It is where your leg joins your foot.

Your ankle is a bone inside your leg.

astronaut

An astronaut is a man or woman who travels into outer space.

Some astronauts have walked on the moon.

apple

An apple is a round and juicy fruit. Apples grow on trees.

Apples can be red or green. Which ones do you like to eat?

awake

You are awake when you are not asleep. Your eyes are open and you know what is going on around you.

Are you wide awake each morning?

baby

A baby is a very young child. Babies do not walk or talk, but they can make lots of noise.

A baby sits in a highchair to eat.

balloon

A balloon is a small, thin bag. You can blow it up with air and make it bigger.

A balloon will blow away if you let go of it.

ball

A ball is round and bounces up and down. You play games like soccer and tennis with a ball.

You have to kick a soccer ball hard.

banana

A banana is a long fruit with thick yellow skin. Bananas grow in bunches on trees.

You pull the skin off a banana to eat the fruit inside.

basket

You use a basket to hold things. Some baskets are made of thin, bendable wood.

Mom puts vegetables and fruits in her basket.

bat

A bat is a small animal with wings. It flies at night.

If you go into your yard when it is dark, you may see a bat.

A bat is a wooden stick. You use it to hit a ball.

You play baseball with a long, thin bat.

bed

A bed is something that you sleep in. Your bed is usually in your bedroom.

Does your teddy bear sleep in your bed at night?

bee

A bee is a flying insect with six legs. Bees can sting you.

Some bees make honey for you to eat.

Bees visit colorful flowers in your garden.

belt

A belt is a long, thin piece of leather or plastic. You wear it around your waist.

You wear a belt to stop your pants from falling down.

a b c d e f g h i j k l m n o p q r s t u v w x y z

bicycle

A bicycle is a machine that you ride on. It has two wheels that go around when you push the pedals.

It is easy to fall off your bicycle when you first learn to ride it.

big

Big means something that is not small. An elephant is a big animal.

If your sweater is too big, it will cover your hands.

bird

A bird is an animal with feathers and two wings. Most birds can fly. Birds lay eggs.

Small birds will come into your yard if you hang out nuts for them.

bite

To bite is to take hold of something with your teeth.

You bite an apple when you eat it.

blow

To blow is to push air out of your mouth.

You blow out the candles on your birthday cake.

boat

You ride in a boat when you travel across water.

The Owl and the Pussycat had a pea-green boat.

book

A book is made from pieces of paper that are joined together. A storybook has words and pictures in it.

Do you like to read a book at bedtime?

bread

Bread is a food made mainly from flour and water. You bake bread in an oven.

You can make toast with a slice of bread.

bottle

A bottle holds liquids such as fruit juice and sauces. Most bottles are made of glass or plastic.

Bottles come in lots of sizes and colors.

bridge

A bridge crosses over a river, a road, or a railroad. A bridge lets you get to the other side.

Cars drive over a bridge, but boats go under it.

box

A box is a container with straight sides. It can be made of cardboard, plastic, wood, or metal.

Do you put your toys away in a box?

bucket

A bucket holds water and other things. It is made of metal or plastic and has a handle.

The bucket of milk has spilled over the floor.

a b c d e f g h i j k l m n o p q r s t u v w x y z

bulldozer

A bulldozer is a very big machine. It can move heavy stones and soil.

You see bulldozers at work on construction sites.

butterfly

A butterfly is a flying insect. It has four colored wings.

A butterfly sometimes spreads its wings in the sunshine.

button

A button is small and usually round. You have buttons to hold your clothes together.

You push a button into a hole or a loop on your shirt.

cake

A cake is made from flour, sugar, eggs, and butter. You mix them together and bake them in an oven.

A birthday cake has icing and candles on the top.

calculator

A calculator is a small counting machine. It can do math very quickly.

A calculator is useful when you have to add up a lot of numbers.

camel

A camel is a large animal with one or two humps on its back. Camels live in hot places.

You can ride on a camel, but it isn't very comfortable!

carrot

A carrot is a long, thin vegetable. It grows under the ground, and you can eat it uncooked or cooked.

Rabbits like to eat carrots.

camera

You use a camera to take photographs. You put a special film in the camera.

Do you take a camera with you when you go on vacation?

cat

A cat is a small, furry animal. It has a long, thin tail and pointy ears.

Do you have a pet cat in your home? What is its name?

canoe

A canoe is a small, thin-shaped boat. You use a paddle to move a canoe through the water.

It is easy to fall out of a canoe, so you need to be careful.

caterpillar

A caterpillar is like a furry worm. Caterpillars change into butterflies and fly away.

Look for a caterpillar on a leaf in your yard.

chair

A chair is something you sit on. Most chairs have four legs and a back.

Goldilocks is sitting in Daddy Bear's big chair.

chicken

A chicken is a farm bird that does not fly. Mommy chickens lay eggs.

A mommy chicken is called a hen, and a daddy chicken is called a rooster.

chocolate

Chocolate is a sweet food. It is made from cocoa and sugar.

Chocolate will get soft and sticky if you hold it in your hands.

clean

When something is clean it is not dirty.

You can make your face clean with a cloth and warm water.

climb

When you climb you use your hands and feet to go up something.

Do you like to climb up the jungle gym?

clock

A clock is a machine that tells what time it is. The clock's hands point to the right time.

An alarm clock makes a loud noise to wake you up.

clown

A clown is a person who dresses up and does funny tricks.

Clowns do silly things to make people laugh.

computer

A computer is a machine that stores lots of information. People use computers in stores, offices, and schools.

You use a keyboard with a computer.

coat

You wear a coat on top of your clothes when you go outside.

A coat keeps you warm when it is cold.

cow

A cow is a large farm animal. Milk comes from mommy cows.

A daddy cow is called a bull.

cold

When something is cold it is not hot. It is cold when there is snow.

Do you get cold when you build a snowman?

crab

A crab is an animal with a hard shell. It has two claws and eight legs.

Have you ever seen a crab on the beach?

a b c d e f g h i j k l m n o p q r s t u v w x y z

crawl

To crawl is to move along on the ground by using your hands and knees.

Babies crawl before they can walk.

crocodile

A crocodile is a long animal. It has lots of sharp teeth and a very strong tail.

Crocodiles swim in rivers in hot countries.

cry

You cry when you are hurt or you feel sad.

Tears run down your face when you cry.

cucumber

A cucumber is a long, thin vegetable. It has green skin and is soft and white inside.

You can cut a cucumber into very thin slices.

cup

A cup is a small bowl with a handle. You put drinks like tea or coffee into a cup.

A cup usually stands on a saucer.

cut

When you cut something you open or divide it. You can use a knife or scissors to cut.

I'll cut the pizza into six slices.

Dd

dark
Dark means that it is not light.

You use a flashlight at night because it is dark outside.

desk
A desk is a table with drawers. A computer sometimes stands on a desk.

You sit at a desk to work.

dentist
A dentist is a person who takes care of your teeth. A dentist can stop your tooth from hurting.

When you go to the dentist you sit in a big chair.

dice
Dice have six sides with different numbers of dots on each side.

You throw dice when you play a board game.

dig

To dig is to make a hole in soil or sand. You can use a shovel to dig.

A dog uses its paws to dig in the yard.

dinosaur

A dinosaur is a very large animal that lived a very long time ago. There are no dinosaurs alive today.

We know that some dinosaurs were as tall as big trees.

dirty

When something is dirty it is not clean.

If your shoes are covered with mud they are dirty.

dive

To dive is to jump into water headfirst. When you dive for the first time it is a little scary.

Penguins can dive into very cold water.

doctor

A doctor is a person who takes care of you when you are sick. Doctors try to make people feel better.

A doctor will visit you if you are in the hospital.

dog

A dog is a furry animal with four legs. Many people have dogs as pets.

Dogs come in lots of different sizes and colors.

dolphin

A dolphin is an animal that lives in the ocean. Dolphins are very smart and are often friendly.

If you're lucky you can see dolphins jumping out of the ocean.

drum

A drum is a musical instrument. You hit a drum with two sticks to make a sound.

I can make lots of noise when I play my drum.

donkey

A donkey is an animal that looks like a small horse. Donkeys have long ears.

Have you ever had a ride on a donkey?

dry

Dry means not wet.

You stay dry in the rain if you use an umbrella.

dragon

A dragon is not a real animal. You can read about dragons in storybooks.

In stories, dragons usually breathe fire.

duck

A duck is a bird that can swim and fly. It has special feet to help it swim.

I like to feed the ducks in the pond in the park.

a b c **d** e f g h i j k l m n o p q r s t u v w x y z

eagle

An eagle is a very large bird. Eagles hunt and eat mice and rabbits.

You will probably not see an eagle in your backyard!

egg

A bird's egg has a hard shell. A baby bird starts to grow inside it. Birds, fish, and insects lay eggs.

A baby chick has to break out of its egg.

ear

An ear is a part of your head. You have two ears, and they help you hear.

You use your ears to hear all the sounds around you.

elbow

An elbow is a hard, bony part of your arm. It is where your arm bends.

You have to bend your elbows when you lift something heavy.

elephant

An elephant is a very large animal. It has big, floppy ears and lives in the jungle.

An elephant is the biggest animal that lives on land.

empty

Something that is empty has nothing inside it.

Your glass is empty when there is no more orange juice in it.

envelope

An envelope is a paper covering for a letter. You put a letter inside it.

You write an address on an envelope and stick a stamp on it.

Ff

fairy

A fairy is not a real person, but someone you read about in stories. Fairies have wings and are often very small.

A fairy waves her wand to do magic things.

fat

Fat means big all over. A fat animal is not thin.

Some monsters are fat because they eat a lot of food.

a b c d e f g h i j k l m n o p q r s t u v w x y z

feather

A bird has lots of feathers all over its body. Feathers keep birds warm. They also help most birds fly.

Some feathers have lots of very bright colors.

fish

A fish is an animal that lives in water. It can breathe underwater. Fish have tails to help them swim.

Some people keep pet fish in a glass tank.

feet

Your feet are at the end of your legs. You stand and walk on your feet.

You have 10 toes altogether on your two feet.

flower

A flower is a part of a plant. Lots of flowers are brightly colored and have a sweet smell.

You can give a bunch of flowers to someone you love.

finger

A finger is part of your hand. You have four fingers and a thumb on each hand.

You can use your fingers to help you count to 10.

fork

A fork has sharp points on one end and a long handle. You use a small fork to eat your food.

You use a big fork to dig in the garden.

fountain

A fountain shoots water up into the air. The water falls down and goes back inside it.

You may get wet if you stand very close to a fountain.

front

The front of something is the part that faces forward. Your eyes are in the front of your head.

A car has bright lights on the front.

fox

A fox is a wild animal. A fox looks like a dog with a thick furry tail.

A fox might look for food in your yard at night.

fruit

A fruit grows on a bush or a tree. Apples and bananas are fruits. Many fruits are juicy and good to eat.

Which of these fruits do you like to eat?

frog

A frog is a small animal that can live in or out of water. Frogs like to live in ponds.

A frog can jump a long way into the air.

full

Something that is full has no space left inside it. You cannot put more into a full glass.

Your glass is full when the orange juice comes right to the top.

a b c d e f g h i j k l m n o p q r s t u v w x y z

Gg

garage

A garage is a building where you keep your car.

Do you have a garage next to your home?

A garage is a place where you take a car to be fixed. You can buy gas at some garages.

A garage has a special machine to lift cars off the floor.

gate

A gate is a door in a fence or a wall. A gate can be made of wood or metal.

You can climb over some gates.

ghost

A ghost is not real. Some people think that dead people come back to visit us as ghosts.

Some ghosts are friendly, but some are a little scary.

giant

A giant is a very big person in a storybook. Giants are not real people.

This giant is even taller than a house.

gorilla

A gorilla is a very big, strong animal. It has lots of hair on its body.

Gorillas live in the jungle in Africa.

giraffe

A giraffe is an animal with a very long neck and long, thin legs.

A giraffe can eat the leaves at the top of a tree.

grape

A grape is a small, juicy fruit. You can eat grapes or use them to make juice or wine.

Grapes grow in bunches.

goat

A goat is a hairy animal with horns on its head. Some goats make milk.

A mommy goat is called a nanny. A daddy goat is called a billy.

guinea pig

A guinea pig is a small, furry animal with no tail. You can keep guinea pigs as pets.

Guinea pigs like to eat lettuce and carrots.

a b c d e f g h i j k l m n o p q r s t u v w x y z

Hh

hand

You have a hand at the end of each arm. Each hand has four fingers and a thumb.

You hold a bat and a ball in your hands.

hat

You wear a hat on top of your head. A hat keeps your head warm and dry.

There are many kinds of hats. Who does the red hat belong to?

happy

Happy means not sad. You are pleased about things when you feel happy.

You are happy if you win a medal on sports day.

head

Your head is joined to your body. Your eyes, nose, and mouth are on your head.

Do you put a hat on your head when you go outside?

helicopter

A helicopter is a machine that flies. It has blades on the top that spin around. Helicopters do not have wings.

A helicopter can fly straight up into the air.

hot

Hot means not cold. When the sun shines you often feel hot.

If you eat very hot food you might burn your mouth.

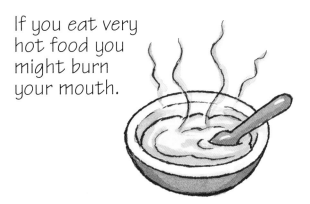

hippopotamus

A hippopotamus is a very large animal. It has short legs. Hippopotamuses like to swim in muddy water.

A hippopotamus can open its mouth very wide.

house

A house is a place where people live. It is usually made of stone, bricks, or wood.

Some houses have rooms on two or three floors.

horse

A horse is a large animal that can run fast. A baby horse is called a foal.

You can ride on a horse or use it to pull heavy things.

hungry

When you are hungry you want to eat food.

Do you feel hungry when it is lunchtime?

Ii

ice

When water is very cold it turns to ice. Ice is cold and very hard.

You make cubes of ice in a freezer.

iron

An iron makes your clothes smooth and flat. You heat up an iron when you use it.

Never touch a hot iron, because it will burn you!

ice cream

Ice cream is a cold, sweet food. It is made from frozen cream and sugar.

What is your favorite kind of ice cream?

island

An island is a piece of land with water all around it.

You can travel all the way around an island in a boat.

Jj

jar

A jar is made of glass or plastic. You keep foods and other things inside a jar.

You can put strawberry jam in a jar.

jelly

Jelly is a sweet food made from sugar, water, and fruit. You can spread jelly on bread.

Do you like to eat grape jelly and peanut butter on bread?

jeans

Jeans are a kind of pants. They are made of a blue material.

Both boys and girls like to wear jeans.

jellyfish

A jellyfish is an animal that lives in the sea. It has a soft body like jelly.

A jellyfish has lots of long, thin legs.

jigsaw puzzle

A jigsaw puzzle is made of pieces of cardboard or wood. You put the pieces together to make a picture.

A jigsaw puzzle can have hundreds of different pieces.

juice

Juice is a drink made from fruits or vegetables. It often comes in cartons or bottles.

You can pour juice from a jug into your glass.

jump

To jump is to leap into the air so that your feet do not touch the ground.

Do you like jumping on a trampoline?

kangaroo

A kangaroo is an animal that lives in Australia. It has very strong back legs so it can hop very far.

A mommy kangaroo carries her baby in a special pocket called a pouch.

key

You use a key to open a door that is locked. Keys are usually made of metal.

You have to turn a key in the lock to open the door.

kick

You kick a ball when you hit it hard with your foot.

How far can you kick a soccer ball?

knee

Your knee is part of your leg. It is where your leg bends.

Dancers have to bend their knees a lot.

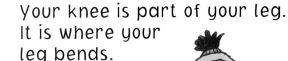

kind

A kind person thinks of other people and helps them.

It is kind to give flowers to someone who is sick.

knife

You use a knife to cut something. A knife has a handle and a blade that is sharp on one side.

A knife can be dangerous, so use it carefully.

kite

A kite is a toy that can fly in the air. It is attached to a very long piece of string.

Remember to hold the string tight when you fly your kite.

koala

A koala is a furry animal that lives in Australia. It has a large, black nose and big, round ears.

Koalas live in trees and like to eat leaves.

ladder

A ladder is a set of steps. You use a ladder to get to high places.

The window cleaner has a ladder to reach the top windows.

lamp

A lamp gives off light. You can switch a lamp on and off.

Do you have a lamp next to your bed?

ladybug

A ladybug is a tiny insect that can fly. It is usually red with black spots.

How many spots can you count on this ladybug?

laugh

To laugh is to make a sound that shows you are happy.

Clowns make you laugh because they do funny things.

leaf

A leaf is the flat green part of a plant. Some trees lose their leaves in the fall and grow new ones in the spring.

The leaves of an oak tree are bright green.

leg

Your leg connects your body to your feet. You use your legs to walk, run, and climb.

You have two legs, but many animals have four legs.

lemon

A lemon is a very sour yellow fruit. Lemons grow on trees in hot countries.

Lemonade is a drink that you make from lemons.

letter

You use letters to make words. There are 26 different letters. Together they make up the alphabet.

You use the letter "j" to start the word "jump."

A letter is a piece of paper with words on it. You send a message in a letter.

You usually put a letter inside an envelope.

light

When it is light you can see what is around you. Light means not dark.

Is it light outside when you wake up in the morning?

lion

A lion is a large, fierce animal that lives in Africa. Lions are a kind of wild cat.

Lions are not friendly animals.

long

Long means not short. A giraffe uses its long neck to eat the leaves at the top of trees.

If your hair is very long it will go past your shoulders.

little

Something is little when it is not big. Little means the same as small.

A sweater that is too little does not fit you very well.

look

You use your eyes to look at things.

A pirate may look for ships to attack.

lizard

A lizard is a small animal with a long tail and four short legs.

Some lizards look like tiny crocodiles, but they will not hurt you.

loud

A loud noise is easy to hear. If you play a drum you make a loud sound.

Do you put your fingers over your ears when you hear a loud noise?

Mm

magician

A magician is a person who does clever tricks. Magicians do magic for us.

Some magicians can make a rabbit come out of a hat.

map

A map is a drawing that shows you where places are. Some maps show you how to get to another city or state.

This map shows you some land with water around it.

make

You make something when you put lots of things together.

Do you like to make things with blocks?

match

A match is a small stick that makes a flame. You rub the thick end on something rough.

You should never, ever play with matches!

medal

A medal is a small circle of shiny metal. You might get a medal if you win a race or do something brave.

This shiny medal is on a colorful ribbon.

milk

Milk is a white liquid that comes from some animals. Cows, goats, and many other animals feed milk to their babies.

Babies like to drink lots of milk.

mirror

A mirror is a special piece of glass. You can see yourself in a mirror.

You can look in a mirror and wave at yourself.

money

Money is metal coins or pieces of paper. You need money to buy things.

Do you keep your money in a purse?

monkey

A monkey is a wild animal with long arms and legs. Monkeys live in hot places.

A monkey uses its hands and feet to climb in the trees.

moon

The moon shines in the sky at night. It moves slowly around the Earth.

The moon is not always the same shape each night.

mouse

A mouse is a small, furry animal with a long tail. Mice can live outside or inside your home.

A mouse can make its nest in a field of grain.

mug

A mug is a big cup. It does not have a saucer. People often drink coffee or hot chocolate out of mugs.

Some mugs have pictures or writing on the outside.

mushroom

A mushroom is a small living thing that looks like a tiny umbrella. You can eat some mushrooms.

It is not safe to eat mushrooms that grow in the woods.

neck

Your neck is the part of your body between your head and your shoulders.

Katie wears a red necklace around her neck.

nest

A nest is a home that birds and mice build. They build nests with twigs, grass, and leaves.

Baby birds stay in a nest until they can fly.

net

A net has a long handle and a soft basket made of string. You use a net to catch fish.

Do you take a net when you go to the beach?

nose

Your nose is on your face. You breathe through it. You also smell with your nose.

You use your nose to find out whether something smells good.

new

New means not old. New things have never been used or worn.

New shoes always look very shiny and clean.

number

A number tells you how many of something you have. You use numbers to count.

Can you see the number 5 in this picture?

newspaper

A newspaper has big pieces of paper that are folded in half. Writing and pictures are printed on the paper.

A newspaper tells you what is happening around the world.

nurse

A nurse takes care of people who are sick. Most nurses work in hospitals.

Many nurses wear white shoes at work.

open

Open means not shut. When a window is open the rain may come into your house.

If the front door is open you can walk into the house.

octopus

An octopus is an animal that lives in the ocean. It has a soft body and eight arms.

An octopus uses its arms to swim quickly through the water.

orange

An orange is a round, juicy fruit. You take off the thick orange skin and eat the juicy part inside.

Oranges keep you healthy, so they are good to eat.

old

Old is not new. Things that people keep for a long time are old. People who have lived for a long time are old.

Old shoes are not as shiny as new ones.

owl

An owl is a bird with big, round eyes. It looks for food at night and catches mice, frogs, and insects.

An owl makes a loud hooting sound at night.

a b c d e f g h i j k l m n **o** p q r s t u v w x y z

paint

To paint is to put colors on a piece of paper or on walls. It is fun to paint a picture.

You use a big brush to paint the walls of a house.

Paint is a colored liquid. It is often kept in small jars. You use paints and a brush to make a picture.

What colors are the paints in this picture?

panda

A panda is a very large black-and-white furry animal. Pandas live in China, and there are not many left in the world.

Pandas love to eat bamboo shoots.

parachute

A parachute is a big piece of cloth. It helps a person fall slowly through the air.

A person who jumps out of a plane wears a parachute.

park

A park is a large area where people can walk and play. It has trees and flowers, and sometimes a playground.

Is there a park near your home?

parrot

A parrot is a bird with very bright feathers. Parrots usually live in warm countries.

You can teach some pet parrots to say words.

pea

A pea is a small green vegetable. Peas are round and they grow inside long, thin pods.

You can eat peas uncooked or you can cook them.

peanut

A peanut is a small vegetable, like a nut, that grows under the ground. It has a soft shell.

Peanut butter is made from peanuts.

pencil

A pencil is a thin stick with black or colored material inside it. You use a pencil to write and draw.

You can use a pencil to write a letter.

penguin

A penguin is a black-and-white bird that lives near the ocean. Penguins cannot fly, but they can dive and swim.

Most penguins live in very cold, icy places.

pie

A pie has pastry on the outside and fruit or meat in the middle.
You bake a pie in the oven.

What is your favorite pie?

pig

A pig is a farm animal with a curly tail and short legs. A baby pig is called a piglet.

Many pigs are pink, but some are brown or black.

pilot

A pilot is a person who flies an airplane. Most pilots wear a uniform.

A pilot uses lots of instruments to fly an airplane safely.

pineapple

A pineapple is a yellow fruit. The skin is hard and prickly, but the inside is juicy and sweet.

You cut off all the skin before you eat a pineapple.

pizza

Pizza is a food with bread at the bottom. It has different things on the top, such as cheese or ham.

Do you like cheese and tomato pizza?

plate

A plate is flat and round, and you eat food from it. Plates come in many different sizes.

Some plates have bright colors and patterns on them.

potato

A potato is a vegetable that grows under the ground. It has a red or brown skin and is white on the inside.

You can make fries and chips from potatoes.

pumpkin

A pumpkin is a large fruit with orange skin. Some people like to eat pumpkin pie.

People make faces on pumpkins at Halloween.

present

You give a present to someone on a special day. A present is usually wrapped in pretty paper.

Do you get lots of presents on your birthday?

puppet

A puppet is a toy that you can move. Some puppets have strings. Some are like a glove that you wear.

You can make this puppet walk, run, and dance.

puddle

A puddle is a little pool of water. There are lots of puddles when it rains.

You need to wear boots if you want to splash in puddles.

push

To push is to move something away from you.

Are you tall enough to help push a stroller?

a b c d e f g h i j k l m n o p q r s t u v w x y z

Qq

question

You ask a question when you want to find out about something. "What time is it?" is a question.

Why?

Children ask a lot of questions that begin with the word "Why?"

quarter

When you share something into four equal parts, each part is a quarter.

Do you cut your apple into quarters?

quick

If you are quick, you do something fast. Quick means not slow.

A quick runner will often win a race.

queen

A queen is a woman who is the head of a country. A queen can also be the wife of a king.

On special days a queen wears a crown on her head.

quiet

If you are quiet you make no noise or only a tiny noise. Quiet means not loud.

Shh! You have to be quiet when a baby is asleep.

Rr

rabbit

A rabbit is a small, furry animal with long ears. Most rabbits are wild, but some are pets.

Rabbits like to eat lots of lettuce.

radio

You listen to music and talking on the radio. A radio is a small machine made of metal or plastic.

I listen to my favorite songs on the radio.

radiator

A radiator makes a room warm. A radiator is made of metal and is full of hot water. It is attached to a wall.

The room is warm because the radiator is on.

rain

Rain is drops of water that fall from the sky. Rain comes from the clouds.

If you are outside in the rain, you will get wet.

a b c d e f g h i j k l m n o p q r s t u v w x y z

rainbow

A rainbow is a thick arch of different colors. You see it in the sky when the sun shines and it rains at the same time.

A rainbow has seven colors. Can you name all of them ?

raspberry

A raspberry is a small red fruit. Raspberries grow on bushes.

A raspberry is very juicy and good to eat.

rat

A rat is an animal that looks like a large mouse. Most rats are brown or black. Some people keep rats as pets.

Rats often live in cities and towns.

read

To read is to look at words and know what they mean.

Do you like to sit in a big chair and read a story?

refrigerator

A refrigerator is a machine that keeps food cold. It is like a metal cabinet and has a motor. We sometimes call it a fridge for short.

Food stays fresh and cool when you keep it in a refrigerator.

reindeer

A reindeer is a big deer with horns. It lives in cold countries. Reindeer horns are called antlers.

Santa Claus has lots of reindeer.

ring

A ring is a thin circle of metal that you wear on a finger. Men and women wear rings.

A ring with a bright stone sparkles.

roller skate

A roller skate is a boot with wheels on the bottom. You can go very fast on roller skates.

You wear knee pads with your roller skates in case you fall over.

robot

A robot is a special machine. It can do some things that people do. Robots help make cars in factories.

Some toy robots can walk and talk.

roof

A roof is the top part of a building. It covers the walls.

Birds like to sit on the roof of a house.

rocket

A rocket can fly straight up into space from the ground. A rocket sometimes takes people called astronauts into space.

A rocket makes a lot of noise when it leaves the ground.

ruler

A ruler is a flat piece of wood or plastic with marks on the side. You use a ruler to draw straight lines and measure things.

Can you draw a straight line without a ruler?

sad

A sad person is not happy. People do not feel good when they are sad.

Some people cry when they feel sad.

sandal

A sandal is a shoe with straps. Sandals keep your feet cool in warm weather.

When you wear sandals you can see your toes.

sail

A sail is a piece of cloth that is joined to a boat. Wind blows into the sail and makes the boat move.

Sails are often bright colors.

sandcastle

A sandcastle is a shape that you make with wet sand. You fill a pail with sand and turn it upside down.

If you make a sandcastle on the beach, the water will wash it away later.

sandwich

A sandwich is two pieces of bread, with a food such as meat or cheese in the middle.

Do you have a cheese and tomato sandwich in your lunch box?

saw

A saw has a handle, a flat metal part, and sharp teeth along one edge. You use it to cut wood and other materials.

You need a big saw to cut through a large piece of wood.

scale

You use a scale to find out how heavy a person or a thing is.

When you make a cherry pie you weigh the cherries on a scale.

scarecrow

A scarecrow is a funny pretend person on a stick. Scarecrows scare the birds away from the farmer's seeds.

A scarecrow usually wears old clothes and a silly hat.

scarf

A scarf is a long piece of cloth that you wear around your neck. It keeps you warm.

Do you wear a scarf when you go out in the snow?

scissors

Scissors have two blades that are joined together. You use scissors to cut paper, hair, and other things.

You can cut a piece of paper into pieces with scissors.

screw

A screw is made of metal. It is like a thick nail, but it is not smooth. A screw joins two things together.

You use a screwdriver to turn a screw round and round.

seal

A seal is an animal that lives in the ocean and on land. It has flippers to help it swim.

In very cold places seals live on the ice.

seat belt

A seat belt is a special strap in a car or a bus. It stops you from being hurt if there is an accident.

When you sit in a car, you must always fasten your seat belt.

seesaw

A seesaw is a wooden or metal plank that two people sit on. Each person sits at one of the ends. When one person goes up, the other person comes down.

Is there a seesaw in a park near you?

shark

A shark is a big, fierce fish. It has lots of sharp teeth and is not at all friendly.

Some sharks are very dangerous and can kill people.

sheep

A sheep is a farm animal with a woolly coat. We get wool, milk, and meat from sheep.

A baby sheep is called a lamb.

shell

A shell is a thin, hard part on some animals. It fits around the bodies of animals such as crabs and snails.

People pick up shells from the beach and take them home.

shout

To shout is to call out very loudly. People often shout when they are angry.

Do you shout to your friends at recess?

shirt

You wear a shirt on the top part of your body. A shirt often has buttons down the front.

People like to wear colorful shirts in the summer.

shower

A shower sprays hot or cold water all over you. You stand under a shower to wash yourself.

People often have a shower before they go in a swimming pool.

shoe

A shoe keeps your foot warm and dry. Shoes come in lots of different colors and shapes.

How many pairs of shoes do you have?

shut

When something is shut it is not open. You cannot walk through a shut door.

Make sure the door is shut when you leave the house!

a b c d e f g h i j k l m n o p q r s t u v w x y z

sink

The sink is the place in your kitchen where you wash the dishes. You fill a sink with water from the faucet.

Do you put your dirty dishes in the sink?

skeleton

A skeleton is all the bones in your body joined together. People and lots of animals have a skeleton.

You have over 200 bones in your skeleton.

skin

Skin is the covering of the outside of your body.

People's skin can be many different colors.

skyscraper

A skyscraper is a very tall building. Most skyscrapers are built in the middle of big cities.

Some skyscrapers are so tall that they seem to reach the clouds.

sleep

You sleep when you are tired. When you sleep your eyes close and your body is still.

The dog likes to sleep in a basket.

slide

A slide has a ladder and a long, smooth part. You climb up the ladder and go down the long, shiny slide.

I like the big slide in the park.

slow

Slow means not fast. A slow person does not move fast.

A tortoise is a very slow animal.

small

Small means not big. Small is the same as little.

I am small, but my mom and dad are big.

snail

A snail is a small animal with a shell on its back. A snail moves very slowly.

Sometimes a snail puts its head into its shell and you cannot see it.

snake

A snake is an animal with a long, thin body. It does not have any legs, and it slides along the ground.

A snake can wind its body around the branch of a tree.

snowman

A snowman is a shape made of snow. When there is lots of snow you can push it together to build a snowman.

A snowman often wears a hat and a scarf, and has a carrot for his nose.

soap

You use soap to wash and to make things clean. You mix it with water. Soap often smells sweet.

You make bubbles when you wash your hands with soap and water.

a b c d e f g h i j k l m n o p q r s t u v w x y z

sock

You wear a sock on your foot. It is made of soft cloth. You put your socks on before you put your shoes on.

Some socks have bright colors and designs on them.

soft

Soft means not hard. Clothes like sweaters and socks are made of soft cloth.

A kitten's fur is very soft.

spaghetti

Spaghetti is a food that looks like long pieces of string. It is hard before you cook it, and goes soft when it is cooked.

It is not easy to eat spaghetti.

spider

A spider is a small animal with eight legs. A spider makes a web to catch flies to eat.

Some people are scared of spiders, but most will not hurt you.

spoon

A spoon has a long handle and a round part at one end. You use a spoon to eat foods such as soup, ice cream, and cereal.

Spoons are made of metal, plastic, or wood.

squirrel

A squirrel is a small, furry animal with a long, fat tail. It loves to eat nuts.

Most squirrels are gray, but some are red.

stair

A stair is a step that you walk up. You have to climb the stairs to get to rooms at the top of a house.

At bedtime I climb each stair very slowly.

starfish

A starfish is an animal that lives in the ocean. It has five arms and looks like a star.

A starfish does not look like a fish at all.

stamp

A stamp is a small piece of colored paper. You stick a stamp on a letter or package before you mail it.

You have to put a lot of stamps on a big, heavy package.

story

A story tells you about things that have happened. Stories are not always true. You can read a story in a book.

The children listen to a story at the end of the day.

star

A star is a small, bright light in the sky. You can see stars at night when it is dark.

There are too many stars in the sky to count them.

strawberry

A strawberry is a juicy red fruit. It is sweet to eat. You do not have to cook strawberries.

Strawberries grow on the ground, so they are easy to pick.

submarine

A submarine is a boat that can move under the ocean. It can also travel along the top of the ocean.

A submarine can dive down very deep.

sun

The sun shines in the sky in the day. It keeps us warm and gives us light.

The sun is like a bright yellow ball in the sky.

swan

A swan is a large bird with a long neck. It lives in rivers and lakes. Swans have big, strong wings.

I like feeding bread to the swans on the river.

sweep

You use a brush to sweep a floor. When you sweep you make something neat and clean.

I sweep the leaves when they fall off the trees.

swing

A swing has two thick pieces of rope or metal, and a piece of wood for the seat. You sit on a swing and make it move back and forth.

If you go very high on a swing remember to hold on tightly.

switch

A switch is what you use to turn things on and off. You press a switch to turn on a radio or a light.

The light goes on when you press the switch.

Tt

table

A table has a flat top and usually has four legs. You sit at a table to eat your meals.

What can you see on top of this table?

tail

A tail is the long, thin part at the back of some animals. A mouse has a long tail. A pig has a curly tail.

A dog wags its tail when it is happy.

tadpole

A tadpole is a baby frog. It lives in water and has no legs at first.

When a tadpole grows legs and loses its tail, it turns into a frog.

teddy bear

A teddy bear is a furry toy. Teddy bears can be small or large, and they are all cuddly.

My teddy bear sleeps in my bed at night.

a b c d e f g h i j k l m n o p q r s t u v w x y z

teeth

Your teeth are the hard white parts in your mouth. You use your teeth to chew your food.

You should brush your teeth twice a day.

telephone

A telephone is a machine that lets you talk to people who are in another place.

When a telephone rings you know that someone wants to talk to you.

telescope

A telescope lets you see things that are very far away. It has a long, thin tube that you look through.

The stars look bigger when you see them through a telescope.

television

A television is a machine that brings you pictures and sounds from other places. We call it a TV for short.

Which shows do you like to watch on television?

tent

A tent is a little house made of cloth. You can fold up a tent and carry it with you.

You can sleep outside in a tent.

thermometer

A thermometer tells you how hot or cold something is. A nurse or doctor may put it in your mouth if you are sick.

A thermometer tells you when a sick person is very hot.

thin

Thin means not fat. A pencil is thin.

The monster has long, thin arms and legs.

toad

A toad is like a big frog. A toad crawls on land, but a frog jumps.

If you touch a toad you can feel the bumps under its skin.

thumb

A thumb is the thick, short finger on your hand. You have two thumbs.

My big brother sticks up his thumb when he wants to say "Yes!"

toe

You have five toes on the end of each foot. Your toes are all different sizes.

Can you wiggle your toes?

tiger

A tiger is a large, wild animal. It is like a big cat with an orange coat and black stripes.

A tiger is a strong and fierce animal.

tomato

A tomato is a soft, round fruit. Tomatoes are red, and they grow on vines.

You can cut up a tomato and eat it in a salad.

a b c d e f g h i j k l m n o p q r s t u v w x y z

tongue

Your tongue is the soft pink part inside your mouth. Your tongue helps you taste your food.

It's a bit rude to stick out your tongue!

toothbrush

A toothbrush has a handle and a small brush at one end. You use it to clean your teeth.

You put toothpaste on the end of your toothbrush.

top

The top is the highest part of a thing. If you walk to the top of the hill you get to the highest point.

She put the box on top of the closet.

towel

A towel is a cloth that you use to dry yourself. Towels are soft and colorful.

Do you have a favorite towel in your home?

toy

A toy is a thing that a child plays with. Dolls, blocks, train sets, and jack-in-the-boxes are toys.

You often keep toys in a toybox.

tractor

A tractor is a farm machine with big wheels at the back. It pulls heavy loads and other machines.

The farmer drives his tractor across the field.

train

A train moves along a railroad track. It has an engine that pulls cars. People ride in a train from place to place.

A train goes fast, so you get to places quickly.

trumpet

A trumpet is a musical instrument. It is made of metal. You blow into one end and sounds come out of the other end.

When you play the trumpet you have to blow hard.

tree

A tree is a tall plant. It has a thick middle part that is made of wood. Many trees have green leaves.

You can pick red apples from this apple tree.

trunk

A trunk is the long nose on an elephant. Elephants use their trunks to pick up food and water.

Elephants spray water out of their trunks.

tricycle

A tricycle is something you ride on. It has one wheel in front and two wheels in back.

How far can you ride your tricycle?

turtle

A turtle is an animal with a hard shell on is back. It can live on land or in water.

A mother turtle often lays her eggs in the sand.

a b c d e f g h i j k l m n o p q r s **t** u v w x y z

umbrella

An umbrella stops you from getting wet when it rains. You hold an umbrella over your head.

Some umbrellas have pictures on them.

vacuum cleaner

A vacuum cleaner sucks up dirt from floors and carpets. It saves you a lot of hard work.

You can clean up quickly if you use a vacuum cleaner.

unicorn

A unicorn is not a real animal. It is a make-believe animal that looks like a horse with a horn on its head.

You read about unicorns in fairy stories.

vase

You fill a vase with water and put flowers in it. A vase is usually tall and thin.

When you pick flowers from the garden you put them in a vase.

vegetable

A vegetable is a part of a plant that you can eat. Potatoes and carrots are vegetables.

Which vegetables do you like to eat?

vet

A vet is a special doctor who takes care of animals. You can take your pet animals to a vet.

If your pet cat is sick you take it to a vet.

violin

A violin is a musical instrument. It has four strings, and you play it with a long stick called a bow.

You hold a violin under your chin to play it.

wash

You wash something to make it clean. You wash your hands with soap and water to make them clean.

Do you help wash the car when it's dirty?

water

Water is the clear liquid in rivers and oceans. Water falls out of the sky as rain.

Water from the faucet has no taste, but water from the ocean is salty.

wet

When something is wet it is covered with water. It is not dry.

You get very wet in the rain if you forget your umbrella.

witch

A witch is a make-believe person in a story. Witches wear tall, pointed hats and fly on broomsticks.

A witch often has a black cat with her.

wheel

All wheels are round and they turn. Wheels help cars, bicycles, and tractors move.

A tractor has big wheels, but a stroller has small ones.

wizard

A wizard is a make-believe person who does magic. You read about wizards in stories.

A wizard can do clever magic tricks.

wind

Wind is air that moves fast. A strong wind blows things around.

The wind helps dry the wet clothes.

write

You put letters or words onto paper when you write. You can write with a pencil or a pen.

She likes to write in her diary every day.

x-ray

An x-ray is a special photograph. It lets a doctor see inside your body. You have to go to a hospital for an x-ray.

An x-ray shows if a bone is broken.

xylophone

A xylophone is a musical instrument. It has rows of bars that you hit with two small hammers.

Can you play a song on a xylophone?

yawn

You open your mouth wide when you yawn. This lets in lots of air. People yawn when they are tired.

You yawn when you are ready to go to bed.

year

A year is the time it takes for the Earth to move around the sun. There are 12 months, or just over 365 days, in a year.

A calendar shows you how many days are in a year.

a b c d e f g h i j k l m n o p q r s t u v w x y z

yogurt

Yogurt is a creamy food that is made from milk. Sugar and fruit can be added to yogurt.

Cherry yogurt is pink and tastes sweet.

young

You are young if you were born a short time ago. Young means not old.

A baby is a young person.

zebra

A zebra is a wild animal. It looks like a horse with black-and-white stripes. Zebras live in Africa.

A zebra likes to eat grass.

yo-yo

A yo-yo is a round toy on a long piece of string. You hold the string and make the yo-yo move up and down.

You need to practice to be good with a yo-yo.

zipper

A zipper joins two pieces of cloth together. Some clothes have a zipper instead of buttons.

I like the zipper on my coat because it is easy to zip up.

The alphabet

a is for apple

b is for banana

c is for cake

d is for dog

e is for elephant

f is for fairy

g is for gate

h is for hat

i is for ice cream

j is for jar

k is for kite

l is for lemon

m is for moon

n is for nest

o is for orange

p is for pizza

q is for queen

r is for rabbit

s is for sandcastle

t is for teddy bear

u is for umbrella

v is for vegetable

w is for witch

x is for xylophone

y is for yo-yo

z is for zebra

Numbers

1

2

3

4

5

6

7

8

9

10

1st 2nd 3rd 4th 5th

Colors

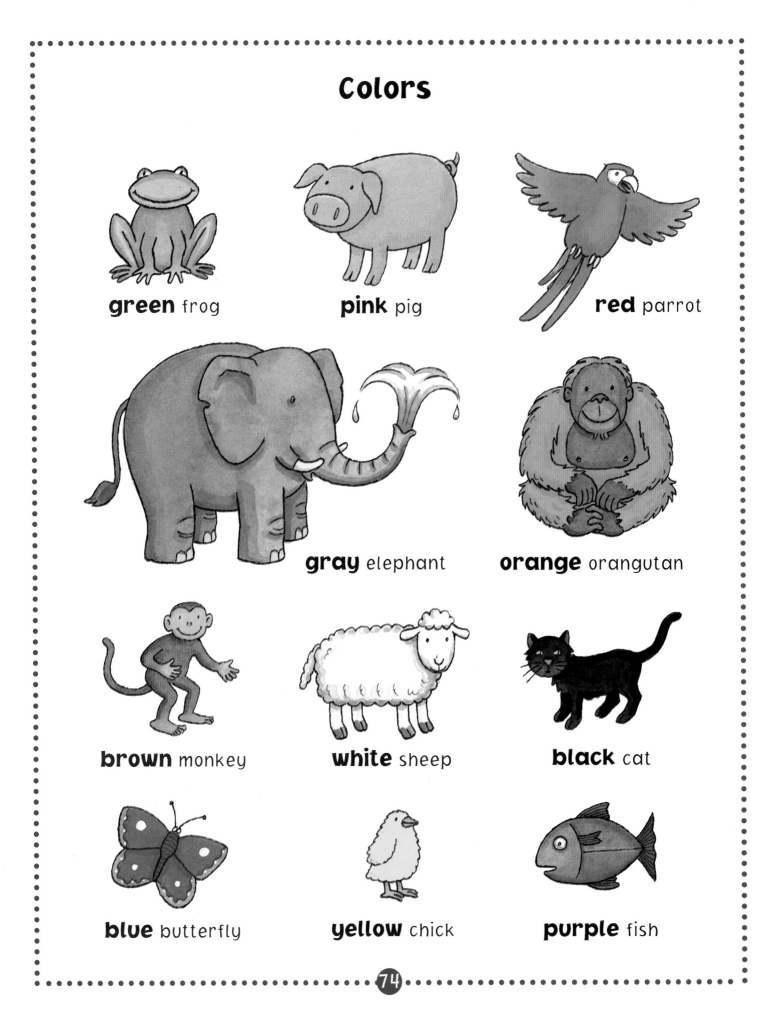

green frog

pink pig

red parrot

gray elephant

orange orangutan

brown monkey

white sheep

black cat

blue butterfly

yellow chick

purple fish

Shapes

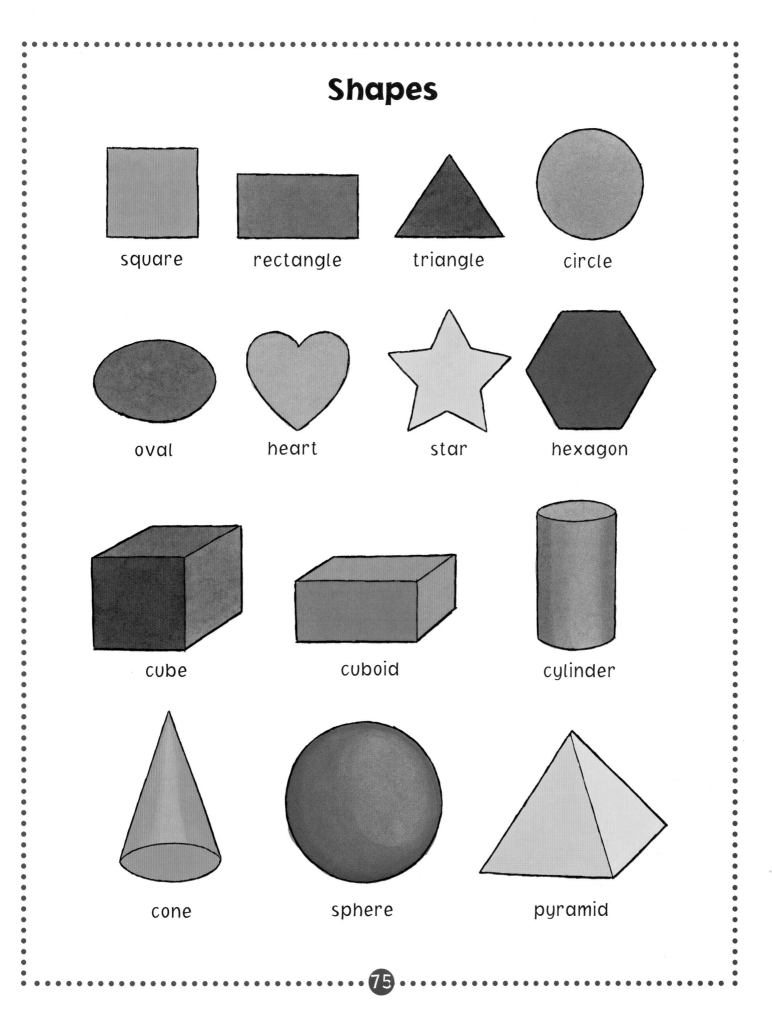

square

rectangle

triangle

circle

oval

heart

star

hexagon

cube

cuboid

cylinder

cone

sphere

pyramid

Opposites

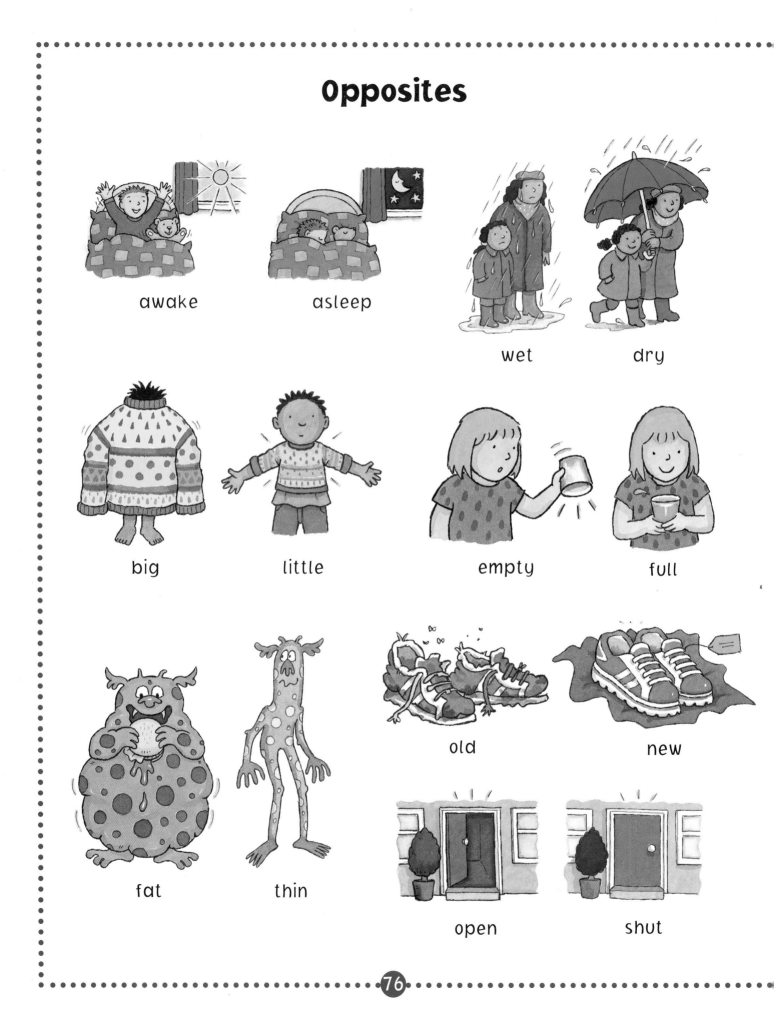

awake

asleep

wet

dry

big

little

empty

full

fat

thin

old

new

open

shut

on   off

out

in

up

down

over

under

above

below

behind

in front of

a b c

f g

l m n

q r

v w x